GW01086452

Note From the Author

This publication is based on real life counselling room experiences. However, some details have been altered to avoid any accidental patient identification. The essence and importance of the issues addressed has remained unchanged.

Acknowledgements

In preparing this book I have spent many hours sitting in front of the computer in complete isolation reliving the times I spent in my session rooms. Not only because some of the cases were tragic and very, very sad, but also because, many times, I had no power to help and couldn't do anything else but send patients off with some hope that there *might* be a solution... Working for an institution has many limitations and the impartiality that a counsellor should have is often in direct conflict with the institution's rules imposed upon you.

Although the content of this book is not vast, the time required to complete first version in 2002 (which was distributed freely to health professionals and patients alike in London, UK where I lived and worked at the time) was well over three months. In that time, my family has had many cold dinners and many incidents where the only answer I could give was: "Please leave me alone." For that, I first have to thank my children for being patient, and understanding that I needed my time. Secondly, my ex-husband, Daryush, for helping and supporting me in many ways, not least of all, the practical help given by typing many versions of the manuscript when my back was hurting or my eyes needed a bit of a rest.

I would also like to thank Dr. David Perry, life-long friend who has coped with my many moods and who was my first port of call in correcting my grammar and sentence structure as my first language is not English (although I would call myself fluent in English).

And finally, I thank Robert Kidd, a professional editor, who showed me that there is much more involved in editing than just looking for good English. It is always painful to see how many mistakes you've made after completing the manuscript and thinking it is ready for publication.

Although I am an academic and have written many scientific papers and revised many Dissertations, I am not a writer. Without all these people to help this project would not have been possible.

I thank you all.

Angie

Preface

Infertility is thought of as a *non illness* or something that *is just one of those things*. Even worst, the medical profession treats it the same way and hence very few countries will offer financial help for treatments or free counselling support before, during or after the treatments. People who are not infertile seldom realise the emotional and psychological problems patients go through. Going through infertility also requires a great deal of time and money and demands a total commitment. It may even become an obsession.

Private sectors are flourishing and infertility has become a big business. This presents even more problems for the patient whose only aim is to have a child and hopefully as fast as possible as for some the age is running out due to age restrictions for infertility treatments. Questions such as: "Which are the best doctors?", or "Which is the most effective treatment?" are foremost in patients' minds and there is nobody to answer those questions.

This book was created to give infertile couples an insight into what other people are going through, to give the medical profession an insight into what their patient may be concerned with, and, hopefully, to promote awareness that Infertility counselling is not just a *luxury* but a necessary step within the treatment. In addition, this would be the first time, in my knowledge, that the problems facing infertility counsellors have been highlighted. These problems need to be understood by patients when seeing a counsellor.

A well-informed patient has fewer disappointments as his/her expectations gathered from media stories or a clinic's promotional material will be looked at with a critical eye, rather than taken at their face value. I hope this book will give the reader a deeper insight into the realistic issues facing infertility patients as well as the professional counsellor dealing with them at the time.

Infertility Basics and Considerations

Even within the medical community and certainly within the wider population, there is some confusion in terminology relating to infertility. I have taken just two definitions from separate sources to demonstrate the confusion that patients and the general public have when learning about the subject.

1. **Infertility**

    a. Primary Infertility: that suffered by a couple that achieves a pregnancy that does not have as a result a normal newborn child.

    b. Secondary Infertility: when, after a normal pregnancy and birth, a new pregnancy resulting in a normal newborn child is not achieved.

2. **Sterility**

    a. Primary Sterility: when a couple, after a year of sexual relations without taking contraceptive measures, has not achieved a pregnancy.

    b. Secondary Sterility: that of the couple that, after having their first child, does not achieve a new pregnancy after two or more years trying.

3. **Infertility (IF)**

The inability to conceive after a year of unprotected intercourse in women under 35, or after six months in women over 35, or the inability to carry a pregnancy to term. Also included are diagnosed problems such as anovulation, tubal blockage, low sperm count, etc.

4. **Sterility**

An irreversible condition that prevents conception.

Notice the variation from different sources. However, in this book Infertility will be referred to as a broad term encompassing both sterility and infertility as used above. I will leave debate about the precise definition of terms to the medical sector.

We have become so aware of Infertility and Infertility techniques in the last ten years, due to sensational publication of unethical practices in various countries, that we often wonder if infertility is on the increase or is it simply our heightened awareness. Statistics tell us that male fertility has fallen, as a result of a reduction in sperm count and sperm motility or due to vasectomies which is now a very common practise in the western world. There are also frequent cases of mature women who decide to become mothers at an advanced age, trying for a spontaneous pregnancy when their fertility has decreased. So, we can safely say that *the number of people seeking fertility (or infertility, whichever used) treatment* is on the increase.

Apart from the above, we find extreme obesity, anorexia nervosa, serious illnesses, alterations of the thyroid, drug and medicine abuse, alcohol and tobacco, and chemotherapy among general medical causes for reduced fertility. Some causes of infertility are male related: alterations in the testicles, obstruction of conducts, prostate pathologies, alterations in ejaculation, or erection and semen alterations. Some are female related: premature menopause, endometriosis, obstructions or scarring of the Fallopian Tubes, uterine and cervical anomalies or ovulation problems. The remaining cases correspond to a combination of causes, with both being responsible in addition to, so called, *unexplained infertility*.

Physical and psychological maturity of the woman means that the perfect age for having children is between twenty-five and thirty although nowadays couples decide to have children later mainly due to work commitments or going into marriage or permanent relationships later in life. Approximately nine out of ten couples of fertile age who have regular sexual relations achieve a pregnancy in the first year. After thirty-five, female fertility drops considerably and, after forty-five, the chance of pregnancy is very small as their ovarian reserve is reduced. Current reproductive techniques, such as IVF (In Vitro Fertilisation[1]) can help women in becoming pregnant and delivering a healthy baby. Furthermore, it is now possible to have a child in cases of ovarian failure or after premature or physiological menopause (usually after a woman reaches age 45).

It is a difficult to decide how old is too old to have a child, as it greatly depends on the individual situation of each couple, their health, physical condition, and other factors. As mentioned previously, we increasingly find that women choose to have children later in life. Of course, we never feel the years passing by and the sudden realisation that our reproductive age has passed is a totally devastating one. Luckily, science today has enabled women to have babies quite late in life. Most reproductive professionals would agree that 50 for the woman would be a reasonable limit for successful fertility treatment. In addition there is a great ongoing ethical debate as to the age limit for using assisted reproduction techniques (such as Egg

---

[1] Fertilization takes place outside the body in a small glass dish.

Donation[2]) to help someone become pregnant. At present, there are many women in the world who have given birth after the age of 55 using this type of treatment. Even men who previously were told that they were infertile (or sterile, as they have a very small sperm count) can now have children thanks to a very advanced treatment called ICSI[3].

Many infertile couples wonder if psychological factors cause infertility. We do not know enough about what effects emotional disorders have on reproduction. Logical inference suggests they may have an influence that is difficult to quantify. Stress or extreme anxiety may have an impact on those patients who fall into the *unexplained infertility* group.

More importantly, couples who want to have children and are faced with a fertility problem should, in my opinion, always be given psychological support as a routine part of their medical evaluation. They may feel they don't need it at the time as they are preoccupied with trying to get pregnant, however they very seldom realise the emotional rollercoaster they are about to embark on when starting infertility treatment. Sadly, many clinics neither appreciate, nor

---

[2] A woman will use eggs from another younger fertile woman to get pregnant.
[3] A procedure where even if one sperm is present can be extracted and injected directly into an egg to create an embryo

understand the real value of specialised infertility counselling. I hope that the information that follows will highlight this need.

Foreword

Those who have suffered infertility know it is a lonely journey. We often believe that our circumstances are different or unusual. We sometimes isolate ourselves because we think there is no one to talk to, no one who could possibly understand, no one to share with. Most often, medical doctors believe that the patients can speak to them openly telling *them* everything. In some circumstances the doctors feel that they *should* know everything.

In reality, however, this is far from the truth. Consultations with numerous patients has led me to the decision to write something to help patients realise that they are not alone in their quest for a baby. Moreover, to help these people recognize that they have a right to speak to someone privately, about absolutely anything they feel the need to, without the added worry that their treatment may be compromised.

I truly believe that the medical profession must be made aware of the diversity of issues that are being discussed at meetings with counsellors. Perhaps then they will realise that it is not always possible for the patient's medical doctor to be involved in every issue.

This is not a highly scientific referenced work, or a case study. One of my goals was to give infertility a recognizable human face and dispel some of the coldness surrounding its perception as a strictly medical procedure. I have tried to convey the human side of infertility in a short, readable paper based on my personal experience that I hope everyone who has a need will be able to identify with.

Dr. A. Stones , Summer 2014

Table of Contents

Introduction

For most couples, infertility is more than just a physical condition. It is an emotional, as well as a social condition, carrying with it very intense feelings. It is important to acknowledge that psychological and emotional responses to infertility vary greatly, as do people's methods of coping with them. Each person has to find their own way of coping with their specific situation. Sometimes, help from an *outsider* might be needed in order to cope with the problem.

Counselling an infertile couple, or an infertile individual, is not an easy task for any health care provider. Infertility is an experience that constantly fluctuates in intensity and direction, so that at different times one may have different needs, and experience different emotions. This I can say from personal experience. Although I had no problem in conceiving my first two children, I have suffered secondary infertility. Thankfully, I have since given birth to a baby boy.

As a consequence of the fluctuations experienced by the individuals the counsellor cannot adhere to any particular *school of thought*, or any particular treatment model. There are no set "stages" in this experience; at one time the erratic emotions can be mystifying and frighteningly intense, at another, one may simply feel numb. There may be moments when being infertile dictates every facet of the person's life, while at other times the same person may have the strength and courage to change the direction of their life. The way a person learns to deal with the experience of infertility will also vary depending on the individual's emotional and physical health and their commitment to treatment. One day a particular strategy may be of great help, later, that same treatment may be entirely useless. At times the belief that the pain of their experience is very destructive may be the dominating thought, but at other times the individual may find it a useful motivating force in their life.

For the above reasons, the treatment approach I take is based on practical applications of my knowledge as a professional, as well as what I have learned from my personal experience. I try to provide not only the gentle support for those in need of such but also a resource of practical, individualized solutions to the patient's situation at the time.

Most people will successfully cope with, or find a solution to, their infertility situation. Unfortunately, there are those who are not so successful.

What Really Happens in

Counselling Sessions?

Having counselled many infertile couples I have observed that infertility becomes an obsession for many people at some point during their lives. Sometimes, just the fact that one cannot have a child becomes the single most important reason for trying to have one. The main reason for this is the strong sense of surprise when confronted with infertility for the first time. Infertility may have been something they never thought about. It may take some time to come to terms with the reality of this problem. One way patients attempt to deal with this crisis is to shrug it off and convince themselves that it is not a big problem. The denial that they ever wanted children in the first place often intrudes itself and hampers the process of dealing with it and perhaps discovering a solution. People may also try to convince themselves that they are too busy, or that it is their partner that wants children now, and not them. However, in most cases they are aware, at some level, that they really do want a baby. For example, a single successful lady in her late thirties suddenly finds the right partner. Just as suddenly, she realises that the reason she never got accidentally pregnant was not due to her being on the pill, for the most part of her life, but that she has a problem. As she puts it:

> Well, I really didn't have time for kids. In fact, even now, I am too busy but M. is desperate and I am really not getting any younger. The truth is, I didn't mind if I had kids or not, but now that I know I have some sort of problem, I seem to really want a baby desperately. I know it is not right, but I can't relax any more when we make love, I just think –Oh God, please let me get pregnant now! Then I think that perhaps I should make sure I had an orgasm as someone told me there is a better chance I will get pregnant if I have an orgasm. But why didn't I get pregnant in the past? I had an orgasm nearly every time when M. and myself made love…I just think there is no point being with M. since he wants a baby and I simply can't give it to him, it seems.

Infertility is often a lonely and confusing battle, and often, in the beginning, the partner who is infertile feels *completely* alone. This feeling compounded by the social stigma surrounding infertility means that few people are able to discuss their experiences openly. Infertility is still a subject that family and friends are likely to feel uncomfortable with, so an infertile person may have very few people with whom he/she can discuss their feelings. This problem can make them feel even more isolated and make the whole experience more difficult to deal with. At the root of these feelings could be the negative thought that they are less than a whole human being, and that they have in some way failed - that they have let themselves, their partner, or their entire family down.

Feelings of anger and sadness are quite common, as are feelings of loss and betrayal. This is particularly true of women, irrespective of whether it is they who are infertile or their partner. Infertility problems have a host of possible causes. It may have started due to wrongly diagnosed or wrongly treated medical problems in the past. It may be the result of feelings of guilt, and transferring the blame to an abortion, or their past promiscuity, as the case below illustrates.

Mr. and Mrs. H. are both healthy and successful. She is an established artist, and he is an investment executive. Both are in their early thirties. There should be no reason for either of them to believe that they should not be able to have children. Madly in love, having "wild" sex, as Mrs. H. explains, and an exciting life altogether, they were looking forward to having a baby born out of their passionate love for each other. But after two years of unprotected sex and no children, Mr. H. had his sperm count checked.

Suddenly the couple's life changed. Mr. H. had a very low sperm count and the couple needed In-Vitro Fertilisation (IVF). Furthermore, Mrs. H. also found out that she had an unexplained infertility problem and gave these details of her experience:

> I didn't think much of it at the start, but my husband was the one who changed. I don't mind. IVF is a very established procedure these days and the doctor told us we'd be fine. But my husband seems to have lost something...Our sex life is, sort of, different...I understood this, but now when we found that I have a problem too he is the one who doesn't understand me...I just don't know what is wrong...They can't find anything in particular wrong with me, but there is something wrong. We've done three IUIs, two IVFs and I just don't think I can take it any more. Maybe it is all these things we did...Maybe this is it...All the wild things we've done...Well, it seems we will not do anything any longer...Wild or not wild...Well, we may not be any longer...

Waiting for treatment, and the continual hope that "this will be the time", can leave your emotions painfully suspended, creating a continual *hoping against hope* attitude. The nature of infertility is such that you may never know definitely whether you are able to conceive, or you may never even know what is causing the problem. The person's grief therefore has nothing to focus on. Constant frustration like this places great strain upon a relationship.

This brings us to a number of important questions: When, exactly is the right time for a counsellor to intervene? At the very start? After the first unsuccessful treatment? Should we be available all the time? Should the infertility clinics impose counselling on the patients?

Most people will resent counselling in the initial stages for various reasons. Perhaps they are still in denial and are convinced that there was a mistake in the diagnosis. Perhaps they don't want to talk about it since they wish to grieve alone. Perhaps the cost of the counselling is daunting. Whatever the reason, I have no doubt that many medical doctors still do not appreciate the value of infertility counselling enough to routinely offer it to their patients at the start of their treatments. If they did, this would not only offer some personal support to an infertile couple starting this unpredictable journey, but perhaps it would also prepare a couple for the possibility of an unsuccessful outcome, and open other possible options for them from the very start.

Once infertility is diagnosed, couples are likely to experience changes in their intimate relationship.

Those changes may include feeling more emotionally distant, or a need to withdraw from intimacy. The pleasurable aspects of sex in the relationship can be lost. Intercourse can begin to seem pointless and one may feel useless and inadequate as a sexual partner. Feelings of guilt and self-blame may also arise, particularly if one of the partners is identified as being the primary cause of the infertility.

Does your partner feel the same way about you, or do they feel deprived of the opportunity to have children? Are they blaming you for this lost opportunity? Perhaps the infertile partner feels he or she should leave the relationship. More frequently, the infertile partner may fear that the other person might leave them. This may be more pronounced in different cultures, where the cultural background has very strong influence on couples.

Mr. and Mrs. M. are from North Africa and are Muslim, which played a great part in the way Mrs. M. perceived her inability to have a child and the consequences her condition may have on her marriage. The males in Muslim communities are expected to be extremely fertile. It is taken for granted that childlessness is usually the wife's health problem. This very simple statement from Mrs. M. says it all:

> If I don't give him a child he will leave me. Please help me! If he leaves me I don't want to live. I have no future!

In the case above, no one questioned the husband's fertility even though he didn't have children from a previous marriage, and the truth of his fertility was not known at this stage. What if he was infertile? In cases of male factor infertility, the first reaction is an unreal shock and alarm that disrupts the life of the husband. He has suddenly been hit in the very core of his being – his male ego. During recovery he usually goes through a lengthened phase of denial. The husband cannot even discuss his problem with his family or friends since he feels this will make him less of a man in their eyes.

Male infertility is often combined with impotency, and may also be a cause of impotency. This becomes a nightmare situation for a man, irrespective of the cultural background. Impotency and infertility is a taboo subject of discussion that may never be accepted by some cultures, and is still not quite an open subject even in the most liberal cultures. In most societies every married couple is expected to have children. Being virile is historically and culturally tied to masculine male self-esteem. So much so that in some cultures, a wife is expected to take all the blame for the lack of children in order to protect her husband's image.

In Western societies, there are more women making a conscious decision *not* to have children for various reasons. Sometimes they simply do not have maternal instincts. Sometimes there may be worry about genetic problems that may be passed on to a child. For Western Societies, the issue of "having children" is becoming an individual choice and not a requirement for a "happy marriage", or a reason for one's existence. Indeed there are many couples that have extremely successful relationships without children. What happens, years into the relationship, when one of the partners has a change of heart?

Mrs. C. was successful, beautiful and very confident. She was also very young, in her early 20s. Unfortunately, there were many mental health related problems in her family, and she was afraid that her child might inherit these problems. In the beginning, her husband said he didn't mind not having children. After four years of marriage, however, Mrs. C. noticed her husband was often making references to having children. Increasingly, she felt insecure in her relationship and was afraid her husband might leave her because of the fact that she definitely did not want to have children. Yet again, this case shows that the fear of losing a partner is very prevalent. Mrs. C. came to the clinic asking about the possibility of egg donation and was very distressed when she told me her story:

> I know you will think that I am probably imagining things, but I *know* that he wants to have a child so much. He says that we can have genetic testing etc. But I just don't want a child with my genes. I

don't know if he would mind if we had an egg donor, but I just know that our marriage won't last without children. Every time when we make love I think that he is hoping I forgot to take the pill, or that a miracle will happen and I will become pregnant. It is terrible. I just don't know what I would do without him. But I don't want a child with my genes! Full stop!

We never heard form Mrs. C. again and one can only hope that the couple came to some mutual agreement. The emotional trauma this young woman was going through, at the time was real and had changed the whole aspect of this couple's relationship.

As seen from the examples above, infertility has a powerful impact on a couple's relationship, and on their feelings about themselves. It affects both partners physically, psychologically, and socially. They experience a roller coaster of emotions; anxiety, depression, anger, shame, and despair often increase and feed on each other as infertility continues, creating considerable stress on the relationship. Many couples begin to feel that intercourse is a chore, and the bedroom becomes a battlefield for the expression of negative emotions. Partners may become aware of an unfortunate loss of spontaneity, as they become involved in medical procedures, temperature charts, and sex on a schedule. It is easy for them to lose sight of themselves as people in a loving relationship. Those aspects of their personality which initially drew them towards each other get lost in the inevitable questions about a very personal part of their lives. The harmony among couples often becomes disturbed because their feelings and their emotions are so out of control.

All this contributes to the stress placed on the individual, and on the couple. This new stress often manifests itself not only in the ways mentioned above, but also in physical ways. It is well documented that stress can cause physical disorders. The stress of dealing with infertility can actually cause more harm and possibly decrease the chance of successful treatment.

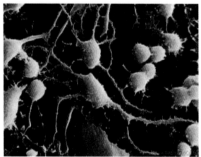

Nerve cells-the mystery of human emotion

People who have difficulty expressing emotion, or those who are unable to assert themselves, are especially vulnerable to stress. Research conducted over the past decade has dramatically demonstrated the direct influence stress and emotions have on the physiological functions of our bodies. With infertility patients, since there no end in sight for their condition, and r guarantee of success, it can often become chronic condition, playing havoc with all aspect of couples' lives. When the goal is to ge pregnant, it is impossible not to feel stress as the months pass by with no pregnancy and perhaps an infertility diagnosis is confirmed. Hope waxes and wanes depending upon what treatment is available, and how long you have been trying to get pregnant. Add to this emotional mixture the real demands of doctor's visits, medications, monitoring, and cost, and it would seem impossible for stress not to enter into the infertility issue.

Even on a very basic level, we know that under stress our sleep cycles are commonly disturbed. People under stress find it hard to have a restful sleep. The resulting sleep deprivation, and insomnia, alters the daily rhythms of several hormones involved in reproduction and fertility. Although very simplistic, this may cause hormonal disturbance, which may, in turn, contribute to infertility. It can become what seems like a never ending cycle of stress and infertility feeding on each other to only make the problem worse.

Does stress cause infertility or does infertility cause stress? Studies on the effects of stress on fertility are limited. Men and women are affected by infertility in different ways. This is related to the traditional ways men and women have been trained to think, feel, and act. It appears that some women with high stress levels may have hormonal changes, irregular ovulation or on occasion, fallopian tube spasm. While the results are inconclusive, recent research suggests that excessive stress may contribute to infertility and pregnancy risks in women. According to Alice D. Domar, Director of the Women's Health Programs, at the Mind & Body Institute at the Harvard Medical School, women trying, unsuccessfully, to become pregnant have levels of stress, in terms of anxiety and depression, equivalent to women with cancer, HIV, and heart disease. Stress in women disrupts the hormonal communication between the brain, the pituitary, and the ovary, interfering with both the maturation of an egg and the ovulation process.

When we are under stress (as is well documented), we experience several neurochemical changes. These changes may be very subtle, or may extend to various mental disorders such as random panic attacks and depression. In some women, even the slightest stress may alter the ordered release of hormones that regulate the maturation and release of an egg. In addition to this, the concentrations of several important chemical messengers involved in reproduction may change as our emotional states change. There is a direct link between the brain and the reproductive tract. Nerve fibres connect the brain directly to both the fallopian tubes and the uterus. The autonomic nervous system influences the ovary's ability to produce healthy eggs and hormones. For example, when a woman is under stress, spasms occur in both the fallopian tubes and the uterus, which can interfere with movement and implantation of a fertilized egg.

New research shows that a common cause of infertility in women, called functional hypothalamic amenorrhoea, or FHA, may be caused by stress. For these women, removing the stress may cure the problem. Women with FHA cannot become pregnant because the hormones responsible for reproduction are not produced in high enough amounts for women to ovulate. Ovulation is the point in a woman's menstrual cycle when an egg is released from her ovary in the hope of meeting a friendly sperm. In this research, a group of women with high FHA have been undergoing cognitive/behavioural therapy. After 20 weeks, all of these women had increased levels of reproductive hormones in their bodies, and 80% actually had the amount of hormones required for the ovulation process to begin. Although the above research does not tell us if these women were subsequently able to become pregnant, the likelihood certainly increased, as they did not ovulate before the treatment.

For men, both physical, and emotional stresses are known to affect fertility. Sperm counts, motility, and structure are altered when under stress. Problems such as impotence and difficulties with ejaculation are often caused by emotional distress in men. Dr. Peri Kedem-Friedrich has devoted 10 years of her research to the possible link between coping with stress, and male immunological fertility problems. She has shown that the way men cope with stress can actually affect their fertility level. Fertility levels improved in those men who had an active coping style, whereas they were weakened in those who respond to stress emotionally. She discovered that infertile men demonstrated lower self-esteem, higher anxiety and showed greater somatic symptoms.

On a physiological level, researchers have recently discovered strong clinical evidence that men diagnosed with infertility have high levels of oxidative stress that may impair the quality of their sperm. Oxidative stress at the cellular level is known to result from many factors, including exposure to alcohol, medications, trauma, cold, toxins, or radiation. Evidence shows that oxidative stress can decrease a sperm's life span, its motility, and its ability to penetrate the egg cell. It is not clear, however, if the stress was due to the infertility diagnosis, or the (temporary) infertility occurred due to a high degree of emotional stress.

It seems from the above that stress can make us less fertile by its effect on our hormones and reproductive organs. The resultant failure to conceive creates further stress, which results in further loss of fertility and so on. This results in a vicious cycle. The circle goes both ways: stress affects infertility and infertility causes stress.

The following example, illustrates the above point very clearly. Mr. and Mrs. T. were married for over 3 years, both in their early thirties and both previously married. Mr. T. had one child from his previous marriage and Mrs. T. had two. They were looking forward to having a child together and saw no problems in starting their new family very soon after their marriage. It did not happen however, and after three years, and a nearly nonexistent sex life in the last year and a half, they approached their own GP. Mrs. T. spoke better English, and after outlining the chronology of the events she asked her husband to go and get her a glass of water as "she was feeling hot and thirsty" (it was summer time and it was indeed hot!) We then had a chance to chat alone for a few minutes. And what a few minutes they were!

> Dr. Stones, you promised that this
> is confidential and I want to tell you
> something very quickly. I don't
> have a period today as I told the
> lady in the scan, but I am pregnant!
> It is not with my husband. I want to
> keep the baby and I don't know
> what to do...

That was a short, cold, and clear statement. The husband came back and we went on to discuss some mundane issues and I asked the lady to see me again after my next appointment, as I wanted to "give her some relaxation techniques" and for that I "needed" to see her on her own! I really couldn't think of any other way to bring the lady back as they were travelling back to their home country the next day. There was no problem with this and while the husband had a "relaxing" time shopping (reverse roles for once!) Mrs. T. (and myself, I must add) had the most traumatic time trying to sort out the best way forward from this very unfortunate situation.

> I don't know what to do now... Maybe you think that because I come from An *open* country I just sleep around, or something...People think that...If we are from Holland we do those things. But people don't! And I am very old-fashioned and I don't sleep around. It just happened...I went to see my ex-husband, since we are still good friends, and I told him how my relationship with my husband is not that good any more because we just have sex to have children and I don't enjoy it, he doesn't enjoy it and so we just gave up enjoying it altogether. And my ex-husband was laughing saying that he can't believe it since he remembers how important sex

was for me when we were together and it just happened...I don't love my ex-husband that way any more, but I really enjoyed sex with him. I didn't think about babies since I couldn't get pregnant for such a long time, he is someone I knew, I didn't have proper sex for such a long time, it just felt like he loved me again and I just felt like a woman again...I don't know. I don't want to excuse myself but I want this child. I think I will just pretend it never happened... Well, I can't even do that since I haven't had sex with my present husband for over five months now and I am nearly two months pregnant. Don't look at me like that, I am not "one of those women"...I don't know why I told you this anyway. You don't know how it feels...

This is a typical example of, not only the *mysteries* of infertility or the infertility that is caused by stress, but also an example of the anger that hides the guilt people are trying to deal with and the terrible secondary consequences of not being able to conceive.

A year later, the couple divorced. Mr. T. has a new partner who is pregnant and Mrs. T. lives alone with her children, but is in contact with both her ex-husbands. Although the relationship between stress and infertility is not entirely known, it is difficult not to believe that this couple's inability to have a child was a result of some form of stress in their relationship caused by a worry that was left unspoken, something kept hidden that they didn't want to talk about or simply couldn't talk about.

What do Infertile Patients

Really Feel?

We have conducted our own research using the Internet, asking infertile couples to tell us about the impact of their infertility (if any) on themselves and/or their relationship with their partner. We have not taken into consideration the duration of infertility, or the duration of treatment. The survey has concentrated primarily on the feelings of the respondents and more complete scientific research is still in progress. All respondents were women and the findings are very similar to my clinical experiences. Five key themes emerged from the data on the respondents' feelings toward their own infertility:

- Failure to fulfil a prescribed social norm

- Attack on personal identity

- Mourning

- Transformation

- Restitution

There are some cultural differences in expressing the feelings, and rationalising the situation, but by and large, the findings concurred with the findings of larger studies in this same area. A letter from one of my patients, who participated in our survey, may echo most of our respondents' feelings and the feelings of many infertile couples. (This letter has been used with full consent of the patient).

> Infertility has changed my relationship with my husband in both positive and negative ways. At the beginning, after we had been trying to become pregnant for about a year, my best friend became pregnant by accident and had an abortion. This brought out intense feelings of jealousy and rage in me at the injustice of my situation - she has choices to have a baby or have an abortion (paid for by the NHS), whereas I have no choice but to spend time and money on trying to have a baby, without any guarantee that I will achieve my goal. My husband could not understand in the slightest what I was feeling or why. For him jealousy is not a natural human emotion, but a shameful and taboo sin. We had a huge row about that, but I think his main feeling is of helplessness and frustration at not being able to solve my problems for me and

make me a happy person again. Somehow, he feels that he is responsible for my happiness, and if he cannot make me happy then he is a failure as a husband, even though the reason for my depression is out of his control. I became unwilling to share my feelings with him for fear of being rejected because of them, since every time I admitted my bitterness about my situation and jealousy of fertile women, it ended in a fight. I eventually turned to a psychologist and also found a support group to help me, and this has succeeded in bringing me and my husband closer together, since he was able to accept the psychologist's word that what I was feeling was normal and ok. He has also met the other women from my support group, and their husbands, and this has made him more understanding and shown him that we are not the only ones with these feelings and going through this trauma. Luckily, our marriage is strong enough that my husband has declared that he wants to stay with me no matter what the outcome of the infertility treatment, so all in all, I think it has

eventually   brought   us   closer
together.

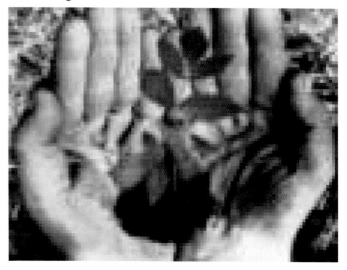

**We must remember that relations are fragile at
the best of times.**

Problems Facing the

Counsellors

To conclude this tour through the infertility counselling room, I would like to draw attention to an additional aspect of the influence of infertility on, not only patients, but also on the other people involved, primarily the counsellors. Stress levels experienced by the people involved in counselling patients with infertility problems are by no means negligible.

Patients who come to infertility clinics come in the hope that they will eventually have a baby. They already know that they have a possible infertility problem, but they do not expect to discover that they have an ovarian cyst, an inverted uterus or in extreme cases HIV. They are offered medical advice, but rarely are they asked if they wish to discuss their condition with a counsellor. They would probably refuse counselling at this time, but they should *always* be told that there is someone they could talk to, even if they feel it is not necessary.

Counsellors are aware of the existence of these patients who may need help but are not offered any and yet we are totally helpless. The lack of knowledge and lack of support by many of our medical colleagues in the infertility sector is a barrier to proper treatment and the help that is available to those who are suffering alone with the burden of infertility. Everyone accepts the role of a counsellor, and yet most don't really understand what this role should be.

When an infertility patient decides to seek a counsellors' help, not only do they seek reassurance and support, they are also seeking practical advice as well as approval for their decisions. In many of the instances, the patient will explore events with the counsellor that cannot be transmitted back to the medical staff, and yet they may have an impact on future treatment management of a patient. This is a great responsibility on the counsellor's shoulders, and carries a real possibility of condemnation from his/hers colleagues depending on how the information is dealt with.

A counsellor working for an institution must adhere to the rules of that institution and is not at liberty to propose any solutions that may contradict the institution's policies. It would be unacceptable for a resident psychologist or a counsellor to exhibit independent initiative without consulting first with their colleagues. Nevertheless, this presents a great burden on any empathic counsellor, since the nature of the profession is such that there is always some element of personal involvement.

Better Times Ahead?

At present, the role of an infertility counsellor is seen, by most clinics, as one of evaluation rather than supportive. As such, the value of such a role is not justly appreciated. There are telltale signs are that this may change in future, and with this, the infertile patients may come to be viewed not just as *patients* but as people who are going through one of the greatest traumas in their lives and need support after medical treatment has been completed. At times, even when the treatment is successful, there is an element of posttraumatic stress which may be disguised in various forms and may linger for a lengthy period. For this reason, continuous support should be offered to patients seeking (or those who have completed) fertility treatment should they need it. Making babies is not a simple, natural task for these patients. Because of infertility it has become a major issue in their lives, and probably the one that will never be forgotten.

14690350R00026

Printed in Great Britain
by Amazon.co.uk, Ltd.,
Marston Gate.